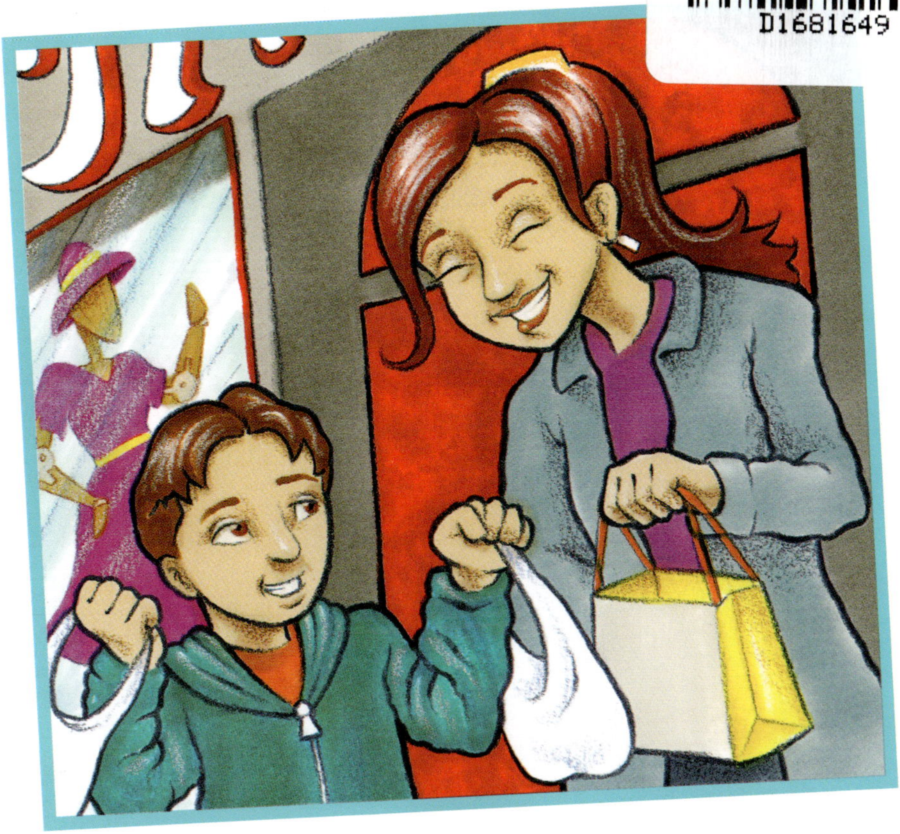

From a Small Town to the Big City

by Brooke Walls

Illustrated by Dan Grant

PEARSON
Scott Foresman

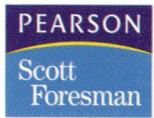

Editorial Offices: Glenview, Illinois • Parsippany, New Jersey • New York, New York
Sales Offices: Needham, Massachusetts • Duluth, Georgia • Glenview, Illinois
Coppell, Texas • Sacramento, California • Mesa, Arizona

Some families live in small towns. Other families live in big cities. Each place can be a great place to live. Each place has good things about it and difficult things. What happens when a family who has always lived in small town moves to a big city? They must get ready for some changes!

In the small town, Josh's family lived in a house. The house was on a quiet street with lots of trees. Josh's house had a yard. This is where Josh and his sister played. Josh's mom had a flower garden.

Josh went to school in the small town. The town had three schools—an elementary school, a middle school, and a high school. All the elementary school children went to the same elementary school. All the middle school students went to the same middle school, and all the high school students went to the same high school.

Most of the time, Josh's family went from place to place by car. Sometimes they walked if something was near their home. They shopped in small stores. Sometimes they went to the park. The town had only one park. The town also had one police station, one fire station, and one public library.

stoop

Josh's mom got a new job in the city. The family had to move. Josh didn't want to leave his friends. He wondered what it would be like to live in a city. Josh was about to find out!

Josh's family moved to an apartment in the city. Many families live in the building. Josh's family has to go up several flights of stairs to get to their apartment. They don't have a yard. They go to the park to play. Now his mom grows plants in a window box. People sit and talk on the stoop in front of the building.

Josh and his family were surprised by the noise of the city. It is very different from the quiet neighborhood in the small town. The streets are busy. You can hear the cars honking: *Honk! Honk! Honk!*

The city has many, many schools for children. Josh's family chose a school for Josh near their apartment. It is a larger school than Josh's school in the small town. Josh's mom says this means that he will have a chance to make more friends!

Josh's family sold one of their cars. They don't need two cars in the city. Instead, they walk where they need to go. Sometimes they take a city bus or a taxi. It seems odd to Josh to pay for a trip. Before, he always rode for free in his mom's car!

---

taxi: a car that people pay to ride in

There are many small shops and even big stores in the city. Josh can't believe how many stores there are to choose from. This is very different from the small town where there are fewer stores.

Josh also visits different parks and libraries in the city. The small town had one of each. He goes to the zoo, the theater, and museums too.

Josh's Small Town and Josh's Big City

	Small Town	Big City
home	house	apartment
school	one per age group	many for each age group
stores	few	many
museum and zoo	one museum and no zoo	museums and one zoo

Josh's life in the city is different from life in the small town. He sees more people. He goes to more places. He hears more noise! But some things are the same. He is with his family. And it is still his job to learn at school and help at home.